Something that can't go on forever, won't.
Economist Herbert Stein

In an earlier Encounter Broadside, I wrote about a higher education bubble – the notion that America is spending more than it can afford on higher education, driven by the kind of cheap credit (and mass infatuation) that fueled the housing bubble.

Nothing has happened to make me doubt that, and, in fact, we're beginning to see universities (like the University of the South at Sewanee and several major law schools) actually cutting tuition, or freezing it, and even reducing enrollments in the face of newfound customer price resistance.

But while the higher education bubble begins to deflate, I think we're also starting to see the deflation of what might be called a lower education bubble – that is, the constant flow of more and more money into K-12 education without any significant degree of buyer resistance, in spite of the often low quality of the education it purchases.

The leading case in point here is the battle over public-employee unions in Wisconsin and elsewhere. And it bodes poorly for the state of lower education. Wisconsin spends a lot of money on education, and its teachers are well paid. The average total compensation for a teacher in the Milwaukee public schools is more than $100,000 per year.

In fact, Wisconsin spends more money per pupil than any other state in the Midwest. Nonetheless, two-thirds of Wisconsin eighth-graders can't read proficiently.

But it gets worse. "The test also showed that the reading abilities of Wisconsin public-school eighth-graders had not improved at all between 1998 and 2009 despite a significant inflation-adjusted increase in the amount of money Wisconsin public schools spent per pupil each year," according to CNS News. "From 1998 to 2008, Wisconsin public schools increased their per pupil spending by $4,245 in real terms yet did not add a single point to the reading scores of their eighth-graders and still could lift only one-third of their eighth-graders to at least a 'proficient' level in reading."

So it's lots of pay but not much in the way of performance. And in this, alas, Wisconsin's situation is typical of public education at the K-12 level around the country. (In fact, one of the reasons given for the increase in higher education costs is the need to provide remedial education for many high school graduates who never managed to learn the things they were supposed to have learned before they arrived at college. It's a shaky explanation for high college costs, but the phenomenon itself is beyond dispute.)

So at the K-12 level, we've got an educational system that in many fundamental ways hasn't changed in 100 years – except, of course, by becoming much less rigorous – but that nonetheless has become vastly more expensive without producing significantly better results.

In the past, when problems with education were raised, the solution was always to spend more money. But as economist Herbert Stein once noted, something that can't go on forever, won't. Steady increases in per-pupil spending without any commensurate increase in learning can't go on forever. So they won't. And as state after state faces near-bankruptcy (and,

---

Steady increases in per-pupil spending without any commensurate increase in learning can't go on forever. So they won't.

---

in the case of some municipalities, actual bankruptcy), we've pretty much hit that point now.

So what does that mean? Well, in the short term, it means showdowns like the one in Wisconsin, where the folks who received those big increases in the past spent over a year raging against the drying up of the government teat.

Getting rid of teachers unions and overgenerous, underfunded public pensions is something states will have to do to remain solvent. But that's just the short term. Over the longer term – which means, really, the next three to five years at most – straitened circumstances and the need for better education will require more significant change.

When our public education system was created in the 19th century, its goal, quite explicitly, was to produce obedient and orderly factory workers to fill the new jobs being created by the Industrial Revolution. Those jobs are mostly gone now, and the needs of the 21st century are not the needs of the 19th.

Perhaps there's still a role for teaching children to sit up straight and form lines, but perhaps not. Certainly the rapidly increasing willingness of parents to try homeschooling, charter schools, online schools, and other alternative approaches suggests that a lot of people are unhappy with the status quo.

Like striking steelworkers in the 1970s, today's teachers' immediate unhappiness may come from reductions in benefits. But their bigger problem is an industry that hasn't kept up with the times and isn't producing the value it once did. Until that changes, we're likely to see deflation of the lower education bubble as well as the higher.

In the coming pages, we'll see how.

In the Beginning

Traditionally, education was not considered the domain of the state. From ancient times, wealthy and middle-class families hired tutors for their children; other schooling was typically provided by parents and religious organizations. For most people, learning was on the job, and they started as children and gradually picked up knowledge about specific skills – farming, shoemaking, merchandising, whatever – along the way. There might be formal apprenticeship structure, or there might not be. Beyond basic arithmetic and writing skills (if that), not much in the way of formal academic training was needed, or obtained, except among the elites.

When our public education system was created in the 19th century, its goal was to produce obedient and orderly factory workers to fill the new jobs being created by the Industrial Revolution.

With the Industrial Revolution, things changed. Industrial-age factories needed workers with more knowledge – and the rapid change brought about by technological progress meant that they needed more abstract skills too. At the same time, older workers didn't want to compete with low-priced child labor, while the Victorian era's more sentimental attitudes toward children made the idea of factory work by kids seem barbaric. In addition, public education was seen as a key component of nation-building. As Ellsworth Cubberley wrote in 1934, the point of public education wasn't that the student would suffer if uneducated; it was that the nation would suffer without compulsory public schools.

The result was the growth of publicly financed and, more significantly, publicly operated school systems. As Seth Godin writes:

Part of the rationale used to sell this major transformation to industrialists was the idea that educated kids would actually become more compliant and productive workers. Our current system of teaching kids to sit in straight rows and obey instructions isn't a coincidence — it was an investment in our economic future. The plan: trade short-term child-labor wages for longer-term productivity by giving kids a head start in doing what they're told.

Large-scale education was not developed to motivate kids or to create scholars. It was invented to churn out adults who worked well within the system. Scale was more important than quality, just as it was for most industrialists.

Of course, it worked. Several generations of productive, fully employed workers followed. But now?

Industrial Revolution schooling involved Industrial Revolution goals and Industrial Revolution methods – organization, standardization, and an overall assembly-line approach. In fact, the industrial-era public school (which persists to the present) is basically an assembly line: kindergartners come in at one end; graduates with diplomas emerge at the other. Each year they advance to the next stage (grade), where the next group of assembly workers (teachers) performs the standardized tasks (curricula) to advance the product (students) to the next assembly stage (grade).

And, as Godin notes, it worked. The growth of widespread public education in the United States was one of the great accomplishments of the late 19th/early 20th century project of elevating the lower classes into a broad-based middle class. It's possible, of course, that we might have accomplished the same thing without government-run schools, but it's by no means certain, and doing so probably would have taken longer and been less encompassing.

But while it worked then, Godin's other

question – "But now?" – is the question for our age. And in a way, it should be no surprise if the next decade or so marks major change. Education is a knowledge industry, after all, and why should we expect a knowledge industry in the 21st century to succeed while following a model pioneered in the 19th?

As Godin says, "Every year, we churn out millions of workers who are trained to do 1925-style labor." That won't work when the kids entering school today will be on the job market in 2025.

The current system isn't working. And, alas, neither are too many of its graduates. There may be a connection.

The Problem

It's no secret that existing schools are under-performing. We keep putting more money and resources into them, but we keep getting poorly educated students out of them.

In 1983 – 30 years ago – the report *A Nation at Risk: The Imperative for Educational Reform* was published by President Reagan's National Commission on Excellence in Education and famously observed, "If an unfriendly foreign power had attempted to impose on America the mediocre educational performance that exists today, we might well have viewed it as an act of war." Since then, things have, if anything, gotten worse. But in the essentials, not much has changed.

There are a lot of reasons for this stagnation. Parents with children care about education, but for the most part, by the time they become aware of problems, it's too late for them to agitate for change in time to benefit their own kids. It's easier to exit the system in favor of private schools, homeschooling, or even just

Why should we expect a knowledge industry in the 21st century to succeed while following a model pioneered in the 19th?

a better school district (though the last option usually requires moving) than it is to effect change. Besides, many parents value school as much as a place to send their kids while they're at work as for any educational benefit. *Those* parents are easy to satisfy. But that's not the only barrier to improvement.

Unsurprisingly, the industrial model of public education has led to an industrial model of labor, complete with powerful unions that make many changes more difficult. Back in the 1930s, the economist John Hicks famously wrote, "The best of all monopoly profits is a quiet life." Change is uncomfortable, and teachers — and, for that matter, administrators – value their own comfort.

There's also a strong current of nostalgia. Parents tend to like the idea of their children's education recapitulating their own. There may be an evolutionary component to that – the cavemen who wanted their children to learn the things they did about finding food and avoiding cave bears were probably more likely to see their genes survive to the next generation – but it's not so adaptive today. Today's parents, after all, are of an age to be products of the very schools that *A Nation at Risk* called "an act of war." Why recapitulate that?

In the 19th century, we needed obedient factory employees who had enough education to execute instructions that were designed by their betters. Today those jobs are mostly gone to China (or to Bangladesh). So we should probably be teaching new and different things. Today's schools, however, aren't even successfully teaching the basics.

What's more, as we've increased the amount of money going in, there's been no corresponding increase in learning. One reason for that is that a disproportionate amount of money has gone into administration, rather than to teaching. According to a report in the *Education Gadfly* describing a study by Benjamin Scafidi called *The School Staffing Surge: Decades of Employment Growth in America's Public Schools*, "Between 1950 and 2009, the number of K-12 public school students increased by 96 percent. During that same period, the number of full-time equivalent (FTE) school employees grew by 386 percent. Of those personnel, the number of teachers increased by 252 percent, while the ranks of administrators and other staff grew by 702 percent – more than 7 times the increase in students."

These education administrators don't teach; if anything, they create paperwork for the people who do. Some of them, of course, are required to by federal regulations, but that hardly improves the situation on the ground. This is one reason more money hasn't improved things: it's not going to teaching but to paper pushing. As Robert Maranto and Michael McShane write, "In constant dollars, education spending rose from $1,214 in 1945 to just under $10,500 in 2008. The St. Louis public schools, for example, spend more than $14,000 per student per year, so if it has problems, money is not one of them. What's far more important is how that money is spent. . . . While expenditures have been increasing over the past several decades, performance has not. The National Assessment of Educational Progress has been given to a representative sample of U.S. students since the early 1970s, and the results have been basically flat. Similarly, the graduation rate for students has remained stagnant, as well, at about 75 percent nation-wide. While some might argue that students today are somehow more expensive to educate, it should be noted that in this time period, rates of child poverty have declined and, in theory, technological advances should have been able to automate and thus decrease the price of some of the processes of schooling."

The problem isn't a shortage of money. The problem is a shortage of value. That is illustrated in the following charts.

First, the United States spends more than many nations whose schools produce better performance. (*See Fig. 1*)

Second, while costs have increased dramatically, performance has not improved. (*See Fig. 2*)

Third, pursuing the politicians' panacea – smaller class sizes – hasn't helped. (*See Fig. 3*)

Adding teachers and administrators has benefited unions (more members) and politicians

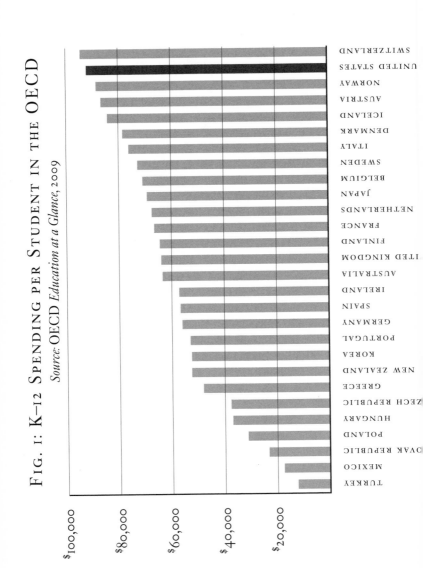

FIG. 1: K–12 SPENDING PER STUDENT IN THE OECD

Source: OECD *Education at a Glance*, 2009

SWITZERLAND
UNITED STATES
NORWAY
AUSTRIA
ICELAND
DENMARK
ITALY
SWEDEN
BELGIUM
JAPAN
NETHERLANDS
FRANCE
FINLAND
UNITED KINGDOM
AUSTRALIA
IRELAND
SPAIN
GERMANY
PORTUGAL
KOREA
NEW ZEALAND
GREECE
CZECH REPUBLIC
HUNGARY
POLAND
SLOVAK REPUBLIC
MEXICO
TURKEY

$100,000
$80,000
$60,000
$40,000
$20,000

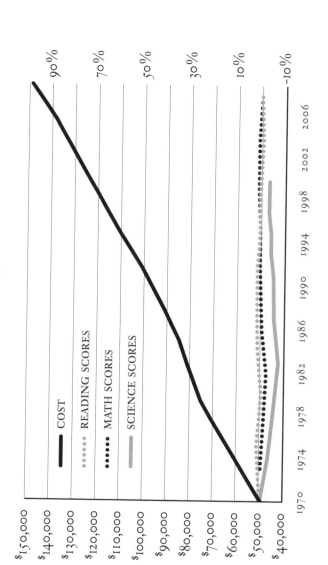

Fig. 2: Real Cost of K–12 Public Education and Percentage Change in Achievement of 17-Year-Olds

Source: Andrew J. Coulson, Cato Institute, based on data from the National Center for Education Statistics

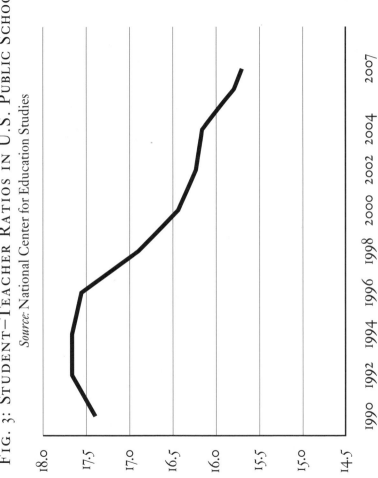

Fig. 3: Student–Teacher Ratios in U.S. Public Schools
Source: National Center for Education Studies

who draw support from those unions (more voters beholden to them), and it has cost a lot of money. What it hasn't done is conferred any measurable benefit on students, who are supposed to be the beneficiaries of public education. And now people have started to notice.

The result is that parents and taxpayers are losing faith in public education. And that portends a potential implosion.

THE IMPLOSION

The New York Times reports that America's largest school districts are seeing devastating drops in enrollment:

> *Enrollment in nearly half of the nation's largest school districts has dropped steadily over the last five years, triggering school closings that have destabilized neighborhoods, caused layoffs of essential staff and concerns in many cities that the students who remain are some of the neediest and most difficult to educate. . . .*
>
> *In some cases, the collapse of housing prices has*

led homeowners to stay put, making it difficult for new families — and new prospective students — to move in and take their place.

But some say the schools are partly to blame. "We have record-low confidence in our public schools," said Kevin Johnson, the mayor of Sacramento and head of education policy for the United States Conference of Mayors. . . . "If we have high-quality choices in all neighborhoods, you don't have that exodus taking place," he said.

The rise of charter schools has accelerated some enrollment declines. The number of students fell about 5 percent in traditional public school districts between 2005 and 2010; by comparison, the number of students in all-charter districts soared by close to 60 percent, according to the Department of Education data. Thousands of students have moved into charter schools in districts with both traditional public and charter schools.

Parents are leaving these school districts because they want better educations for their children. But the consequences for the districts can be devastating.

First, the students who are leaving are probably better than average because their parents care so much about their educations. That means that when they leave, the overall quality of the remaining students, and thus the schools, will drop.

Second, funding is often based on the number of pupils in the schools, so when these students leave, the schools have less money. Since it's hard to get rid of teachers, they'll probably cut "plus" programs like music, art, etc. – but losing those will make the schools less appealing to students who are thinking of leaving, probably accelerating the trend.

Third, parents – that is, taxpayers – who are sending their kids elsewhere (especially those who are homeschooling or sending their kids to private or online schools) will probably be less willing to support taxes for the benefit of public schools they're not using and probably don't think highly of. And, for that matter, once public schools are no longer seen as a near universal institution, taxpayer support in general is likely to fall off. That, of course, means schools will be less funded, which will probably encourage still more students to depart and cause more parents to resent paying taxes for public schools their kids don't use, in a vicious circle that produces shrinkage year after year.

At the moment, it's not too late to change

The current system isn't working. And, alas, neither are too many of its graduates.

---

public schools for the better. But that window will soon close, as the reputational hit they've taken over the past couple of decades continues to sink in. If that happens – and every force in the system, from administrators to teachers unions to the politicians who depend on their votes, is in favor of the status quo – then we'll see increasing numbers of parents voting with their feet, and a true K-12 implosion will set in.

Some people are more optimistic than

ENCOUNTER ⚓ BROADSIDES®

AMMUNITION FOR SERIOUS DEBATE.

Available as eBooks
visit our website at www.encounterbooks.com

To order, contact Perseus Distribution
at 1-800-343-4499; or email
orderentry@perseusbooks.com

For Publicity, contact Lauren Miklos
at 212-871-5741; or email
lmiklos@encounterbooks.com

others. While visiting at Stanford University's Hoover Institution, I spoke with a couple of their experts on educational reform and got two different takes.

Terry M. Moe, a professor of political science at Stanford and a senior fellow at Hoover, is gloomy about change from within. The essence of the American political system, he argues, is checks and balances — and those checks and balances make it easy for people to block change. With too many established interests vested in the status quo, political change is pretty much hopeless, he says. Instead, change will come because of technology. Educational technology, via things like online schools, the Khan Academy, and more, is making big waves. And because it's often both much cheaper and better — and because Americans love technology and politicians oppose it at their peril — this technological revolution will overturn things from without.

Eric Hanushek, a senior fellow in education at the Hoover Institution, was more hopeful about political reform. In a recent book,

Schoolhouses, Courthouses, and Statehouses: Solving the Funding-Achievement Puzzle in America's Public Schools, he outlines ways in which school financing can promote reform. He thinks pressure from parents, and the threat of competition, may be enough to drive change. Teachers unions are a powerful voting bloc, but they're outnumbered by parents.

Both Moe and Hanushek also noted – as did several other people I spoke with in Palo Alto – the strong interest in new education platforms by a variety of start-ups. Many of these are focusing on college and graduate study, but others are working on K-12 education, and some of the approaches blur the line between the two. And with this degree of interest by start-ups, we're likely to see more ferment in the future.

It seems clear, at any rate, that things can't go on as they have. Something that can't go on forever, won't, and we can't go on pumping more and more money into education while getting the same (or less) out.

So what's next?

The New Public Education

The truth is, nobody knows exactly what comes next. And that may be because nothing in particular is coming. That is, instead of replacing our monolithic public education system with something equally monolithic, we may wind up replacing our current system with a whole lot of different things, a variety of approaches tailored to children's (and parents') needs, wants, and pocketbooks. That may not be so bad.

One fast-growing area is online education. Already, over 1.8 million K-12 students are enrolled in online schools, most of them in high school. Online school — at least for those students with self-discipline — can be far more efficient than a brick-and-mortar school, and that efficiency opens up other opportunities for learning.

My daughter did most of her high school online, after spending one day in ninth grade keeping track of how the school spent her time. At the end of eight hours in school, she concluded, she had spent about 2 ½ hours on actual learning. The rest was absorbed by things like DARE lectures, pep rallies, and other non-academic activities. Instead, she enrolled in Kaplan's online college-prep program, where she was able to take a lot of Advanced Placement classes not offered in her local public school and where the quality of instruction was higher overall. (In the public school, she reported, her science classes spent a lot of time on the personal difficulties the scientists had had to overcome; at Kaplan, the focus was on their great experiments and why they were important.)

The flexibility also allowed her to work three days a week for a local TV-production company, where she got experience researching and writing for programs shown on the Biography Channel, A&E, etc., something she couldn't have done if she'd been nailed down in a traditional school. And she still managed to graduate a year early, at age 16, and head off to a "public Ivy" to study engineering.

Did she miss out on socializing at school? Possibly, but at her job, she got to spend more

At the moment, it's not too late to change public schools for the better. But that window will soon close.

time with talented, hardworking adults, which may have been better. (And, as a friend pointed out, nobody ever got shot or knocked up at online school.)

Is online school for everyone? Absolutely not. Some kids don't have the discipline to sit down at a computer every day and do school-work with no one looking over their shoulder. (I'm not sure that I would have at that age.) But for the right kids, the online approach offers benefits that traditional school doesn't.

The Khan Academy follows a different approach, in which lecture-type materials are done online at home, while students work on problem sets and get one-on-one help from teachers in the classroom. This is currently undergoing in-school testing at several locations, but I spoke with one ninth-grader whose school is part of the program, and she reported that it's been terrific for her. She always found math difficult and scary, but now, she says, it makes sense and is much less frightening.

Some children benefit from a Montessori approach that allows kids to follow their own interests and work at their own pace. Other kids benefit from a more rigidly structured traditional approach. Still others do best with homeschooling, which seems to be enormously beneficial for many kids when their parents are willing and able to invest the effort. (Look at how many homeschoolers win the National Spelling Bee.)

Given that there are so many different kinds of kids and, today, so many different kinds of career paths, it makes sense to allow different approaches. This isn't the industrial age anymore. Why pursue a one-size-fits-all approach in education?

At the moment, we do that because we've always done it that way. This is an odd approach, given that education is sold as the ticket to

America's future. If that's true, why be guided by the past?

There are, at any rate, two ways in which things can go forward. On the one hand, these new and innovative approaches can take place within the context of publicly funded education. On the other, they can be embraced by parents who are fleeing what they regard as a failing public system.

From the standpoint of public schools, the former approach is infinitely better. If parents are free to choose different approaches according to their situations and their children's needs within the public school context, then those parents (and other taxpayers) will see public education as delivering value for their money. And while parents will remain supporters, the children will continue to keep enrollment numbers up for the systems, keeping the public money flowing as well.

On the other hand, if the only way parents can avail themselves of these new approaches is to exit the public school system, then they are likely to be resentful of the taxes they pay.

And if enough people exit the public schools for other environments, taxpayers in general may come to regard public education as, essentially, just another program for the poor. That's likely to mean a steadily decreasing willingness to provide financial support, especially in times when there is competition from other budget priorities.

Which approach will win out? At this point it's hard to say, but here's one indicator: more and more public schools are offering online programs of their own, usually through a national vendor like K12.com. Sometimes these programs are designed to accommodate kids who are physically unable to attend school or who have behavioral problems. But they're also appearing now as genuine alternatives. School systems like it because online education is cheaper, leaving them with more money to spend on other things. And many parents and students like it because of the flexibility.

Flexibility may be a hidden payoff of a more open approach to public education in general. It's easy to miss just how many rigidities are introduced into American life by the traditional public school approach, but those rigidities are legion. Getting rid of them may help address other problems.

Real estate prices, for example, are heavily influenced by the quality of local public schools.

For the right kids, the online approach offers benefits that traditional school doesn't.

Poor people often can't afford to attend top-flight public schools because they can't afford to live in the district. People who own property in those districts, meanwhile, stand to lose a significant amount of their home's value if the school board rezones them into a district with less-favored schools. Often people are forced to live in areas they'd otherwise rather not — because of long commutes, for example — simply in order to avail their kids of a decent education. By cutting the link between location and school quality, those problems could be eliminated, likely resulting in substantial savings.

Kids, too, would get additional flexibility. As I mentioned, one of the great fringe benefits of my daughter's experience with online school was that she was able to hold down a job. She spent 12 hours a week working at a TV-production company, doing work that ranged from the semiglamorous – doing research and writing treatments for shows that aired on Biography and A&E – to the not glamorous at all, like filing videotapes, processing expense reports, and making coffee.

That experience was enormously valuable to her. Few other kids have two years of high-

This isn't the industrial age anymore. Why pursue a one-size-fits-all approach in education?

level work experience at the age of 16, and she learned not only specific skills but also the broader talents of working in an office and getting along with people. That was huge, and it's not the kind of thing you learn when cooped up in a building with a bunch of other teenagers. (Perhaps most valuable, she got the experience of sorting the résumés sent in by people applying for jobs. That teaches things that can be learned nowhere else.)

I frequently hear employers complain that entry-level employees, even in their 20s, don't really understand how to operate in a work environment; all they've ever known is school, and school is an unnatural environment. A more flexible approach to public education might help address this by allowing more teenagers to get work earlier. Many education reformers have talked about the value of apprenticeship-style models; it's a lot easier to do that sort of thing when you're not stuck listening to DARE lectures all day.

*   *   *

CONCLUSION

With the federal government strapped and with many states and municipalities looking at budget cuts and even bankruptcy, spending on K-12 education can't continue increasing at current rates. It particularly can't continue increasing at current rates when the results remain so dismal.

Something that can't go on forever, won't. So these educational trends won't continue indefinitely. What will we see instead? Based on what we know to date, it seems likely that a new solution will be one that is:

1. *Cheaper.* Costs are out of control, and taxpayers are out of money. Stopping the runaway increases will be the first priority, but over the mid- to longer term, school systems will be looking for actual savings. There's no reason, in an age of exploding information technology, that the United States should be spending so much more than other countries to educate its kids.

2. *Better.* Current education isn't just expensive; it's also not very good. Despite high per-student spending, U.S. students lag behind other countries. Much time in school is wasted, and the smarter kids are often held back by classes that are designed not to leave the slower kids behind.

3. *More flexible.* Accommodating the districts, schedules, and other requirements of public school systems introduces all sorts of costs and distortions into other parts of life: real estate prices, commuting patterns, and the ability of teenagers to seek gainful employment. This one-size-fits-all approach may have made sense 100 years ago, when society was simpler and alternatives were scarce. It doesn't make sense anymore.

4. *More diverse.* Speaking of one size fits all, the old-fashioned approach of treating students like interchangeable parts in an industrial-age machine doesn't fit

with the wide variances among students in abilities, learning styles, and interests. Again, 100 years ago it may have made sense to take our square-peg kids and educationally hammer them into societal round holes. Today, not so much. In our more diverse society – and economy – it makes more sense to let kids learn in ways that play to their own particular strengths.

5. *More parent-friendly.* With smaller families the norm and with changing societal attitudes toward parenting, many of today's parents are more involved and interested in their kids' educations. These parents aren't happy just shipping their kids off to an educational warehouse for the day. They want to know what's going on and to take a hand in directing things.

Given these characteristics, perhaps it makes more sense to speak of *solutions*, rather than *a solution*. Rather than looking for the one best way to educate our kids, we might be better off putting together a diversified portfolio of educational approaches, some of which work better for some kids in some circumstances and some of which work better for other kids

---

I frequently hear employers complain that entry-level employees, even in their 20s, don't really understand how to operate in a work environment; all they've ever known is school.

---

in other circumstances. Such an approach is likely to produce better outcomes, and at lower costs.

But given that something that can't go on forever, won't, one thing is certain: change is coming to public education, and in a major way. Educators would be well advised to move with the tide, rather than trying to stand against it.

First American edition published in 2013 by Encounter Books,
an activity of Encounter for Culture and Education, Inc.,
a nonprofit, tax exempt corporation.
Encounter Books website address: www.encounterbooks.com

Manufactured in the United States and printed on
acid-free paper. The paper used in this publication meets
the minimum requirements of ANSI/NISO Z39.48 1992
(R 1997) (*Permanence of Paper*).

FIRST AMERICAN EDITION

LIBRARY OF CONGRESS CATALOGING-IN-PUBLICATION DATA

Reynolds, Glenn H.
The K-12 implosion / Glenn Harlan Reynolds.
pages   cm
ISBN 978-1-59403-688-0 (pbk. : alk. paper)
ISBN 978-1-59403-689-7 (ebook)
1. Public schools—United States. 2. Education—Aims and objectives—
United States. 3. Education—Social aspects—United States.
4. Education—Economic aspects—United States. 5. Education—
United States—Finance. 6. Education and state—United States.
7. Educational evaluation—United States. 8. Educational change—
United States. I. Title.
LA217.2.R49 2013
371.010973—dc23
2012046709

10 9 8 7 6 5 4 3 2 1